The Hanging Tree Has No Leaves

Pamila Miller Ndanyi

Edited by Dr. Sonia Cunningham Leverette
Cover Illustrated by Lee Anthony Williams

Published by Hadassah's Crown Publishing
Simpsonville, SC 29681

Text Copyright © 2018 by Pamila Miller Ndanyi

All rights reserved. No part of this book may be reproduced, scanned, or distributed in any printed or electronic form or by any means without prior written consent of the publisher, except for brief quotes used in reviews.

Please do not participate in or encourage piracy of copyrighted materials in violation of the author's rights. Purchase only authorized editions.

Library of Congress Control Number: 2018953389

ISBN 978-9981230-9-7

Printed in the United States

Disclaimer- Police in this country are necessary, as they serve a wonderful purpose and truly help save and attempt to maintain the peace. But, when numerous unarmed young men are shot and killed unjustly, this is wrong. It's wrong when police are given paid time off while a young man's family is paying for a funeral. Time and time again these officers are found not guilty of shooting kids, teens and young adults, often in the back, while they are unarmed. The system is broken and the African-American race is targeted unjustly.

Dedication

This book is in memory of my parents, for instilling God, family and a great work ethic in my soul. Many thanks also go to Reverend Dr. Marcel Bush and the Majority Baptist Congregation for believing that this book was possible, my children and grandchildren, who I love beyond words, and finally, but never last, my sister Sherry, my rock, my confidant and the best person I have ever known.

Table of Contents

A Poet's Thoughts on Social Justice

Pain	11
Put Down the Guns	13
The Hanging Tree	14
Building Hope Off Broken Words	15
Border Tears	17
RISE UP!	19
Black Men	21
Have You Ever Wondered?	22
Hidden	24
Hiding	25
Notice Me	26
I Can	27
Black Girl	28
Beware	29
Kindness	30

A Poet's Thoughts on the Seasons of Life

Glory Walk	33
Live	35
Dreams	36
Death	37
Life	39
Signs	40
Good Stewards	41
At the Gate	43

A Poet's Thoughts on Family, Home & Love

Bless	47
Mother	48
Father	49
Mama	50
Papa	52
Daughter	53

Baby Boy	54
Grandchild	55
Brown Child	57
Rose	58
Dancing	59
Newberry	60
Home	61
Christmas Time	62

A Poet's Thoughts on the Majesty and Effects of Nature

Snow Fall	65
Chirping	66
What Spring Brings	67
New Birth	68
Horses	69

A Poet's Dramatic Presentation of the Three Wise Men

The Bright Star	72
First Wise Man	74
Second Wise Man	77
Third Wise Man	79

A Poet's Thoughts on Social Justice

Pain

We will never know your future.

We will never know your child.

The pain of this heartache will never,

never subside.

The beauty of their faces

The kindness in their hearts

The love of family and friends

With shattered and broken hearts

How many more must suffer this terrible

heartless act?

How many more must be taken away before

our leaders react?

Will it take a rain of bullets to shatter their

children's lives,

Creating a killing field in schools with blood running

from side to side?

Stop the killing this heartache brings.

Stop it before it's too late.

Help our children live out their lives,

help them to see another day.

Note
This poem is in remembrance of shooting victims throughout the land.

Put Down the Guns

Young men! Young men! Put down the guns.
You choose a weapon that is all wrong.

Again, and again, we are putting you in the ground,
Or sending you on a bus ride to prisons out of town.

Many of you leave behind children that suffer,
Or you leave behind a mourning mother.

Put down the guns and pick up a weapon,
The only weapon that promotes intelligence.

Pick up a book and improve your life.
A gun only creates heartache and strife.

Don't give the man a chance to cut short your life;
Erase your number from the prison cell life.

Remove the headstone from a grave too soon;
It's never too late to choose the right thing to do.

Put down the guns and make your life last.
Live to be an old man with a history,
not a young man with a prison past.

Live to tell your children about yesteryear,
Not visiting the graveside of a parent that's not here.

Put down the guns and tell the story of young men
who made it, not for fame or glory,
But for men who lived to tell their story.

The Hanging Tree

There's a hanging tree; it is not in the ground.
It has no leaves.

The branches are real and are used to kill
On these hanging trees.

People are around and they look on.
But, no one can help once the victim is gone.

Bullets now take the shape of the tree.
Young innocent youths shot down in the street.

Branches carefully extend their arms
Letting loose a hail of bullets 'till the victims are gone.

Or, a sheet may be used to hang them in a cell.
The jail is not safe for black people to dwell.

The hanging tree has been replaced.
It shadows a rope with a gun in its place.

Hate lives on for the Black race,
While juries are consistently saying, "not guilty" today.

Beware my people, don't you see,
the hanging tree has no leaves.
The shadow of a gun is what you'll see.

Building Hope Off Broken Words

As the next generation, you guys are the hopes and dreams of
the African American race.
You are our future and you will form our past.
What you say, what you do, what you think will be recorded.

Have HOPE that everything you reach for will come to you.
Have HOPE that you will tread a path that will make it easier
for the next generation to follow.
Have HOPE that you will be that example that turns others
around.
Have HOPE that you will be that bright and shining star that
leads the way.

While you are shining, while you are leading the way,
do not be discouraged.
Do not be led down a path of false promises or empty words.
Some of us African Americans do not know or have forgotten
the hardships and sacrifices that have come before us
Slavery, lynching, rapes of our great,
great, great grandmothers, aunts and cousins,
selling of their babies and the lashes
of a whip across our forefathers' backs,
left to bleed and wear the scars for the rest of their lives...

Do not be easily persuaded by a hotdog, a soda or a few nice
words used to tamper down unjustly wrongs.
Do not be persuaded by a night out of frivolity that so easily
turns the heads of many.
Remember that we are men, women and children.
Remember that we bleed red.
Remember that we cry real tears.
Remember that our children, fathers, sisters
and mothers are being hurt and murdered

by the very ones that offer a hotdog, a soda and empty words
that end on the same note of black intolerance and the
shattering sounds of bullets as they hit a falling body.

The TIME for silence is coming to an end.
The TIME for new leadership is past.
We as a people have leaned on Martin L. King Jr.
long enough.
We as a people have allowed the
negro race to slide backwards.
Our black men are increasing the prison population,
while decreasing their lives,
their family units and their educational opportunities.

What am I HERE to tell you today?
I am HERE to tell you to fight for what you want,
Not with fists or ugly words, but with wit and brains.
Speak out and speak up.
Do not be afraid; you guys are the leaders of tomorrow.
Don't be fooled by empty words or promises.

March, if you have to.
Raise your voice; use your vote.
Raise hell if you have to, but raise it in the right way.
Use your voice; use the vocal strength of many.

But DO NOT let your voices
or your vote become SILENCED!

Border Tears

I never thought I would see this day,
when America would go back in time
when the shame of America's history
would once again shine.

Lest we not forget, the days of slavery time,
when children were sold away from their parents,
and the ones who sat on high,
did not see this as a crime.

Has lady liberty covered her eyes,
to helpless children in need?
Do the strongest powers in America laugh
and shout with glee?

Is this how we make America great again,
on the tears of children who want to come in?
Lest we not forget America's
shameful Native Americans' "trail of tears."

When America's flag flies,
she beckons for those to come in…
The hungry, the poor, the tired,
the children she would take in.

Lest we repeat America's terrible past,
of ripping children from parents' arms
from those who loved them first
and those who'll love them last.

May the flag continue to wave,
the huddle masses in.
Let us not forget the shame,
when these terrible crimes began.

The taking of the children,
branding them for all time.
Or do we record in history
"The Year of The Border Crimes?"

RISE UP!

Each day I watch the news
and each day I hear a voice inside me
saying, "RISE UP,"
Not in hate or bitterness or rebellion but in LOVE.
Love for the people that came before me,
For their tears and fears, their struggles and hurt.
Love for the road that they walked,
the fight that they fought
Love for the injustice they felt.

RISE UP and
let your voice be heard.
Speak the truth and don't be afraid.
RISE UP and say
we have a president who wants to take us back 400 years.
RISE UP and know
that these are our brothers and sisters
who are being deported.
These are our brothers and sisters
whose synagogues are being bombed,
For it wasn't that long ago that our churches were
and still are being burned.
It wasn't that long ago
that we lost four angels
in a bombing in a black Alabama church.

RISE UP and know
that we are still being murdered,
RISE UP and remember Sandra Bland.
Remember that a lie killed Emmett Till,
a fourteen-year-old young black man,
and that same lie could murder you today.
We are a people who will not listen,

will not learn from the past,
who will not embrace each other,
will not heed the Word of GOD.
Many times in the Bible,
the Lord, God sought to teach his people
a lesson to get their attention.
Donald Trump is our lesson!

RISE UP when you have a chance.
Use your voice!
Use your vote!
RISE UP as a people of color
and know that we have a long and rocky road.

Rise UP and know
that we have not overcome,
but we can overcome!
RISE UP and know
that separate we are one,
but together we are strength.

The battle is the Lord's,
but through Him He has given us a voice,
a power, a strength that we can and will
RISE UP, for we will NOT go backwards.
We cannot continue to lean on the ones that are GONE,
REV. MARTIN LUTHER KING JR., ROSA PARKS,
OUR PARENTS AND GRANDPARENTS and
many more who fought the fight of bigotry, racism and hate,
FOR THEY ARE TELLING US…
RISE UP!

Black Men

Black men! Black men hear my cry,
the time for action is here and now.
Get off the street corner; there is nothing there
Don't go on the porch and have a seat.
Don't walk the streets; there's nothing to see.

Black men! Black men take care of your home.
The children are crying; there's no food at home.
Don't run to your homies.
Some are drunk, drugged or dead.
But, stand like a man and hold up your head.

Black men! Black men, you're important and strong
With an education, you cannot go wrong.
Leave the streets and the corners alone
Leave the drugs and the homies,
Take care of home.

Have You Ever Wondered

Have you ever wondered how the slaves felt,
as they were forced away from their land?
How the sounds of the chains clanked,
as they shuffled through the sand?
The sounds of the cries from the one's left behind,
an empty mother's hand?
Can you hear the wailing sounds
resounding from the Mother Land?

Have you ever wondered what despair the slaves felt,
as they lost sight of their land?
How the sounds of a foreign tongue increased,
their hopeless fears and pain
The clanking sounds of the crying slave child,
shackled down in iron chains
No mother to dry their tears or a father to break the chains.

Have you ever sunk to the pit of despair,
not knowing what tomorrow brings?
To be in the pit of a belly's ship
that's slowly shattering your dreams
The sounds of the water as it hits the ships sides
The moans of the sick and the dying.

Have you ever wondered what it would be like
to be ripped from your mother land?
To be chained, beat and starved
not knowing where the ship will land
The sounds of the songs coming from the belly,
the moans of a hopeless man.

Have you ever wondered what it would be like,
to be stripped from your birth land?

Have you ever wondered why the slaves survived
after being ripped from their mother land?

Why the moans and cries turned into chants
as the ship steered toward new land
Why the darkness gave rise to an enslaved people
down in the pit of the belly
Why the chains, the chants and the songs that were forged
still rise from the ship's dark belly.

Hidden

I have faced racism and stared it in the face.
I know for a fact racism has a place.
It lives in the heart of a hidden face.
I know for a fact racism has a face,
A subtle yet quiet hidden face.

I know that racism has a place
A smirk of a smile
Well-chosen words,
A write-up for something that was only heard.

Racism thrives and is alive and well
Its birth and bred then rears its head
A burning cross, a strong limbed tree
A history of racism the South decreed.

Racism is not gone, it's here to see.

Hiding

Turning deep within myself
Peering from behind a wall
A façade of being brave and strong

Longing to hear a familiar word
A soothing touch upon my face
Comforting arms, a long embrace.

My wall is strong.
It took years to build.
My wall protected me
So that I could live.

I'll hide and I'll peer.
I'll keep them all out.
My wall was strong
To keep them all out.

My wall has cracked.
I no longer peer.
I see the light of what I feared.

I'll keep my wall ever so near,
which I used to hide and peer.
I'll keep my wall ever so near.

Notice Me

Sitting at the city square
I look around and see
the people passing in a hurry,
but no one notices me.

I might as well be a tree
Standing thick and strong
My limbs outstretched reaching to the sky.
My leaves holding strong
But, no one seems to notice the beauty of my tree.

Maybe I will be a bug crawling all about.
Will someone swat or step on me,
then make me a gooey ink blot?
No, they will never notice a crawling bug like me.

I know, I will flit and flutter just like a butterfly.
I will light on their nose or maybe even their toes.
Then maybe someone will notice.
I'm a pretty butterfly.

No, I think that I will just be me,
A fat, little round bumblebee.
Maybe I will sting one, two or three.
Then I bet someone will notice me.

I Can

I am a black woman! Smart and proud.

My voice is soft, strong but not loud.

I hold my shoulders back and erect

A sign of my blackness that I respect.

I speak with the confidence my parents instilled

Fighting the battle, only climbing up hill.

My arms are long with the thickness of my race

A honey brown that reflects in my face.

The thickness of my hips, my thighs and my legs

No way defines my place in this race.

I can do anything, I can go anyplace.

My intelligence as a black woman cannot be erased,

A soft but confident black woman I am.

My expression of blackness that says, I can.

Black Girl

'They" say things have changed but I say not really.

There is a niceness in the air, a bit of civility.

Hey black girl, stay in your place.

You will never be as smart as this white race.

Don't overstep being a negro girl

Corporate is a place for the white world.

Don't overstep; stay in your place.

Your opinions will be tolerated, but not taken at face.

Advancement is merely done for numbers.

Hey black girl, it's not your time or number.

"They" say that things have really changed.

I say look under the shade, things are still the same.

There is something new that this black girl can see.

There's a new rope that hangs from the tree.

Beware!

Beware! Of words that cause divide
Silent signals given in the name of pride.

Beware! Of those that step on your rights
The right to stand or kneel in pride.

Beware! That your voice is not silenced or stomped
Trampled or cut down to a political romp.

Beware! Stand strong, let your voice be heard.
Take a knee, take a seat, it's your right to be heard.

Kindness

The longer I live
The more I see that
Kindness is deep and
It comes from within.
It can be faked but
It won't last long.

For the truth of kindness
Is very strong
A simple touch
To soothe a sadness
A silly hug to generate laughter
A listening ear to an elderly couple
A sandwich given to a homeless person
A simple gesture is all it takes.

Kindness is a character
That cannot be taught.
It's there;
It's inside of you.
It comes deep from the heart.

A Poet's Thoughts on the Seasons of Life

Glory Walk

I walked this earth as a humble man,
never knowing what tomorrow would bring.
A dedicated soldier, working on my Savior's team
As I walk this road to glory
I'll stop and reflect on some things.
Did I sing of the Lord's glory?
Did I praise his holy name?

As I took another step on this road to glory walk,
I heard my mother's voice,
"Come home my son, your work is done,"
a smile came over me.

A little further as I walked, I could hear my family cheer,
"Welcome home, dear brother,
we've been waiting for you here."
I never faltered in my steps,
my walk was as good as new.
All sickness washed away from my body;
my body was brand new.

My earthly life disappeared with each step that I took.
I stopped to look back-- to say goodbye;
I knew it was my final look.
The gates opened wide as I stepped inside,
and my Savior took my hand.

He said to me, in a voice that pleased,
"You've sung my songs, praised My name,
you've helped your fellowman.
Heaven is your home, your work is done,
you've entered the promise land."

Note

This poem is dedicated to a man who stopped to welcome a weary stranger home. He offered a smile and invited her to his home church, never knowing they would meet again, on the front steps of Majority Baptist Church, where he greeted her again with a smile and a welcome to come on in. Rest in Peace, Mr. Melvin Hardy.

Live

Once I am buried do not linger
Hang around or stay
For life is not at the grave side,
But outside of this place.

Remember all the fun times
A few of the sad ones, too
For life is not about grieving,
You must live your life through.

Talk about me sometimes.
Do not let my memory fade,
For memories replace grieving,
As slowly as time passes away
A smile will take grief's place.

I'll love you guys forever
Death does not take love away
So do not stay or linger
At my grave side today.

Live, love and smile.
Do not let my death take that away.
Hold my memories in your heart
As you live your life every day.

Dreams

Crossing the river of my dreams,
Skipping pebbles and watching them gleam.

Reaching for the stars, forever looking forward,
This train is on the track of success and reward.

All aboard, all aboard this choo choo train,
Uphill, uphill, I have everything to gain.

Look ahead and grab with both hands,
Pick up and start any unfinished plans.

The world is full of hope and dreams,
I am taking the reins; I am going full stream.

I can do it. I can make. I can cross the river,
There is no turning back, not now, not ever.

Death

Death has long been a friend of mine.

Some say she's harsh, but I say she's kind.

She waits with patience in the shadows.

Death is at the bedside, there when it matters.

With the gentlest of hands, she reaches out with a touch.

She removes all the hurt, the pain and suffering.

She releases the soul from a tired or wrecked body.

A sweet release to our heavenly father.

Death is on time for a soul that is ready.

She is on time, even if we're not ready.

The sweetest of smiles, serene and mellow,

She places her hand on the soul that is ready.

Off she goes as they walk side-by-side.

To start the next journey on a heavenly tide.

Death is not harsh; she is a friend of mine.

For death is certainly always on time.

Life

During difficult times when life is full of misery and strife

Reach back and grab a memory

when life was good and sweet.

Grab on to that memory, grab on and grit your teeth.

Never stop believing in all your hopes and dreams.

Remove all negative thoughts and

dismiss those that don't believe.

Age does not matter to fulfill your hopes and dreams.

The only thing that matters is the happiness that your life brings.

Signs

A chill in the air, the weather is changing
Cool wet dew on the ground
It's light sweater season.

Vibrant color of leaves floating on air
Golden yellows, oranges, browns and reds
Resting now on a grassy bed.

The rustling of falling leaves to the ground
Natures patchwork blanket forming her crown
To protect her seedlings on the ground.

Orange pumpkins, red apples, yellow-golden and green,
Ready for pies,
a true sign that autumn baking season is here.

The scratch of the rake as it gathers the leaves
The sounds of the children as they jump in the heaves
enjoying the crisp, crunchy sound
of the raked bundled leaves.

The smells, the sounds, the early morning chill
Light sweaters, warm apple pie and cider to drink
These are all God's signs that autumn season is here.

Good Stewards

Someone should take a peek inside,
the Good Stewards on watch
do not abide the careful spending of what's inside.

Who's watching the watchers,
spending the cash of the hard-earned citizens
who have retired at last.
Promises made, often broken,
never a word allowed to be spoken.

Are corners cut on food and care?
Is there enough staff to comb mama's hair?
A shortage here, a shortage there,
the Good Stewards know what the families don't know.
Shush be quiet, it remains unspoken.

A beautiful building shadows what's real.
Look beneath the cover to see the real deal
A lack of nurses, CNA's too,
struggling to give the care that the aged are due.

The aged, the gems in their final years are short-changed
the care that is due to them.

The Good Stewards are paid to provide good care,
families should peek beneath the flare.
The staff's not at fault as it always seems.
Check out adequate staffing,
which makes a great team.

The pearls of my life are before me
with each step that I take,
The glorious pearly staircase leading to my fate.

The bottom step glowed clearly with flashes
of my childhood years.
A tire latched to a tree and me swinging happily.

A few more steps revealed my early teenage years
A time when my Lord was important.
A time when I held church dear
Family and friends were important;
they influenced my teenage years.

At the Gate

As I climbed the pearly stairway,
I feel no despair.

Images flashed before me of dear ones I've left behind,
babies growing big and strong,
families reaching milestones.

Praising the Lord every day,
for faithfully guiding my family's way.

Goodbye my family,
it's time to go.
I must continue my climb.

We will meet again someday
at the pearly, heavenly gate.

A Poet's Thoughts on Family, Home and Love

Bless

Lord, bless my family as we gather in your name,
to eat and laugh and pray.
Allow us to stand in your presence
as we share this blessed day.

Remove old grudges and negative thoughts.
Replace them with happy times.
As our hands prepare this bountiful food,
let your Holy Spirit surround me and mine.

Bless large and small, short and tall
Bless each of us in your way.
Teach us Lord to love,
as you love each of us every day.

Bless this day, oh mighty Lord.
Bless it in your name.
We humbly ask of you Father, to let your spirit reign.
For on this faithful Thanksgiving Day,
shower us with blessings in your name.

Mother

What is a mother, does anyone know?
Does she wear a hat with a big red bow?
Does she wake you early to go to school?
Does she check your book bag for left-over food?
Is mother the one who washes the clothes,
   cooks the food and wipes your nose?

Does she laugh at her jokes and cry at sad movies?
Or is she the one with extra wide arms that hug us and rock us and
   keep us from harm?
Does she give you the look
   when she knows that you're wrong?
Does she read her Bible and pray over you?

When we fall, is she the one with an outstretched hand?
Is mother the one that gives sound advice, like
"Hold steady my child, it will all be alright."
Is she the one we always count on?
The go-to person during happy times
Or the run-to person when the world lets us down?
We know that mother is this much and more,
   for the word mother is truly adored.

Well, mother dear, I want you to know,
   it does not matter how much I have grown.
It does not matter how far I roam,
   or if the Lord has taken you home.
When I see or imagine a smile on your face,
   then the world for me is a much better place.

Father

I placed my hand in my father's hand and
walked along his side
A giant of a man, I thought,
bigger than life to me.
He pushed me in the right direction and
taught me responsibility.

A man who taught me right from wrong, who
instilled in me hope and pride.
He said, "Hold your head up high,
step on no one
And speak with the voice of a queen."

My father's gone, but until I leave,
I will remember my hand in his…
the lessons he taught me
about hope and pride,
but much bigger,
he taught me responsibility.

Mama

I remember mama,
and the light upon her face
the early morning light,
showing her beauty, her style her grace.

I remember mama,
and the lines around her eyes,
from sitting with her sick child,
for hours during the night.

I remember mama's touch
with hands rough and worn
working from sun up to sun down,
to care for those she'd born.

Washing clothes and donning socks,
cooking cakes and pies,
never taking time for self,
not even to dry her eyes.

I remember mama
cooking over the old, white stove
cooking and stirring, these things she did,
things she did with love.

Sunday dinner was a must, a treat for all of us.
The smell of fresh fried chicken,
black eyed peas and collard greens,
steamed brewed tea, drifting through the house
to feed her
Family.

I remember mama reading words to me.

She'd pick up her old worn Bible,
she's had since she was three.

The spoken Word of God she said,
was passed down to me
to you, my children
quiet now and listen to me.

Yes, I remember mama
and the light upon her face.
the early morning light showing
her beauty, her style, her grace.

Papa

If I could reach into heaven and shake my father's hand,
he would be so proud of me for the woman that I am.

There are so many memories of my father,
his love and thoughtful care,
from lacing up my shoestrings to washing
and shampooing my hair.

The memories that I hold between these years,
are precious and dear to me,
of a man who sacrificed many things
to make life good for me.

If I could reach into heaven
and shake my father's hand,
the sky would pour tears of joy
for his wonderful, courageous man.

A man who provided protection,
who guided me through the years,
who helped to mold me from a girl,
to the woman that I am.

Daughter

You rarely ever smile these days.
I cannot remember your laugh.
Your heart weighs heavy from the present
and remnants of the past.
Your eyes have lost their luster.
The shine is barely there.
Your pain is growing daily but,
sweetheart you know I care.

You're not a failure at what you do.
In fact, you've done your best.
At some point, we must turn them loose
and pray for the best.
Look in the mirror daily and see what I see,
the strength of many wrapped in one,
the courageous mother of three.

Be still your heart, they will find their way
With many ups and downs.
Know in your heart you've done your best
They must now do the rest.
No words will soothe your troubled heart
or take the pain away
Just know that time will heal your pain
and your smile will return someday.

To my daughter, the teenage years of your children will either
make you weak or stronger.
I see the strength growing in you daily
and someday you will, too.

Baby Boy

Sweet baby boy in my arms,
as I look down at your face
my heart swoons with joy
as I place you down to sleep.

My toddler has grown so fast.
I hear his footsteps running
The peal of laughter at his side,
The pat-pat of his feet running.

The fifth grade is a changing time.
There's a maturity in his face.
Teachers and friends are a part of his life.
He's growing at such a fast pace.

Sixteen years can be a turbulent time
To find out where you stand
pick your friends wisely, my son,
you will soon be a man.

A young man of twenty, he has lost his way.
My hand can no longer guide,
influences of the outside are now
where his time resides.

My sweet young man, as I look at your face.
My heart continues to swoon
but instead of laying him down to bed
I now lay him to rest in his tomb.

Sweet baby boy, I tried my best
to love you and guide your way.
The path you chose took its toll.
Sweet baby boy, take your rest.

Grandchild

The love of your child can make your heart beat

and pound in your chest.

But, the love of a grandchild has its own beat,

as they lay their head upon your breast,

a glance, a touch are all that it takes.

The grandparent is forever hooked.

When I see my grandchildren coming my way

with a smile and squeezed-tight hug,

I would never take a million bucks to trade

for that kind of love.

Admiration in their eyes as they slide their hand in mine,

remembering special times as we walk

in the garden side by side.

"I'll pick you a flower grandma," is what the little ones say.

"This flower is just for you. And did I tell you, by the way, Grandma, that I love you?"

Brown Child

Watching her through clear brown eyes,

A pretty brown light-skinned child

Eyes that hold a mystery

A voice with little sound

A heart that needs mending

Her soul is lost and found.

Hear her anger, although there are no words.

What has happened to this small, light-skinned little bird?

Her mother says, "Leave, get out of my house.

I don't care where you go! Just get out of my house!"

Unspoken anger hears her cries.

What has happened to this pretty,

brown light-skinned child?

Rose

My love for you is like the rose that grows on the vine.

The thorn is just a symbol

that reminds us that pain passes with time.

The gentle curl of the rose petal,

reminds me of your lips

that quiver when the wind blows or after a soft gentle kiss.

The silkiness of the petal is warm like your skin

a velvety smoothness of your body,

as we lie skin-to-skin.

The folds of the petals curling back onto each other

the folding of our bodies as we spoon before we love

the sweet smell of your body, heady like the rose

filling my senses with the fragrance

of the sweet smell of your love.

Dancing

I feel a song dancing in my heart;
It lifts my spirits
and revives my soul.

I dance along the fine line of notes
twirl and spin,
spin and twirl
dancing to the songs of my soul.

Newberry

If the world could see all our hidden gems
We would be amazed at some of them
Tucked away in the south midlands
Surrounded by evergreens and cinder block buildings.

There's a hidden gem that some know about,
It's not rich or poor but there's love all about.
The sounds of laughter, chatter and giggles,
Peel through the air going from the middle.

A bustling, hustling class exchange
Where education is the key and forever reigns.
The college is small but their heart is tremendous,
Nursing welcomed us in knowing very little.

A beautiful college serene and peaceful
Lying in the south of the midlands region.
There are wolves all around
they mean you no harm.

The charm of the school is the wolves baying alarm
Where education has reigned for hundreds of years
Where caring and love is part of this peaceful,
serene atmosphere.

Home

South Carolina is my home.
It's where I want to live
Basking in the sunshine,
frolicking downs the hills.

Laying in the hammock, staring up at the sky
Images of the blue ridge mountains
fresh air on the mountain high.

Dreaming of Myrtle Beach,
the waves rolling through
sand between my toes
the taste of salt on my tongue.

The hustle and the bustle of Columbia's multitude
The southern charm of gentlemen,
as they say, "Hello, how do you do?"

South Carolina is my home.
It's where I want to live,
forever on my mind,
from sea to shining sea.

Christmas Time

Oh! Christmas time, Oh, Christmas time
What a wonderful time of the year

A time when family is celebrated
A time that's full of cheer

Bells ringing, children singing
Stockings stuffed with joy

Christmas lights gleaming bright
Carolers singing "Silent Night"

Wrapping paper glittering on boxes big and small
Gleaming colors from the tree shining for one and all

Hot chocolate by the fireplace, the smell of roasted nuts
Ham baking in the oven, rolls with a buttery touch

The family in a circle, heads bowed in prayer
Giving thanks for this holiday season, love is everywhere

The smell of Christmas is in the air,
Stockings hung on the mantle
Christmas time, Oh! Christmas time,
The best time of the year.

A Poet's Thoughts on The Majesty and Effects of Nature

Snow Fall

Watching the snow fall from my window,

Carolina snow white as cotton

Floating on air as light as a feather

Creating a vision of pure delight

Small snowflakes and large ones, too!

Swirling to the ground to form a bed

Beds of flaky, white cotton snow

A winter wonderland for all to behold

A wondrous gift of flaky, white snow

Creating a playground for young and old.

Chirping

I hear the birds chirping from my window tree

A true sign that spring is coming

The rebirth of what's to be

The singing of the birds

Sweet calls out to me

The freshness of the air as the leaves flower the trees

Calling, calling out to me

The sweet sounds of the birds

Telling all who will listen that spring time is for love.

Chirping birds are calling,

announcing the coming of spring

A time to rebuild, refresh and live

A newness of what spring time offers and gives.

What Spring Brings

Walking through the forest on a clear spring day
the smell of fresh pine cones, gently leading the way
wild iris growing freely,
their orange leaves as bright as the sun.

Worker ants building new forts, a top red-brown stone
stopping to sit by the babbling brook,
shiny rocks aglow,
listening to the gentle sounds of water as it flows.

Watching as spring rebuilds its life,
new patterns as they grow,
sparrows gently stacking their nests,
readying for hatchlings to grow.

Thick brown brush slowly turning green,
providing shelter from within,
nesting warm and cozy bunnies to make a family den.

The forest is full of wonder,
a great place to play and dream,
walking through the forest exploring
what spring time has to bring.

New Birth

Blooming of the white buds on the Bradford pear
A crisp breeze blowing the March spring air
Increased activity on the southern city square
The clock chimes down, evening is near.

The band strikes up a bluesy, soulful song,
Inviting the crowd to dance along.
The slowness of the city, the calmness of the square,
Explode with new birth circling in the air.

New pink and white buds on the azalea bush
Spring grass growing at an alarming rate
The chatter of neighbors as they emerge from their dens,
Happy that winter has come to an end.

Blooming daffodils bright as the sun
Glorious laughter as the littles run
Winter has finally come to an end
The new birth of life now begins.

Horses

Black and white horses rearing their heads
Saying one thing and meaning another.
Bicolored horses rising from the past,
Whining and neighing, the peace will not last.

Black and white colts born to the present
Learned nothing from the horses, no valuable lessons.
Neighing and whining these colts of the present,
tread down the same path, ignoring past lessons.

Bicolored horses, black and white ones, too
All tread the same dirt-trodden path
Not correcting the course of a rugged terrain
Stamping and tramping the dirt from the past
Not running together to create a new path.

A Poet's Dramatic Presentation of the Three Wise Men

The Bright Star

Cast: Father

Siblings (between the ages of six and ten)

Angel on high

Three wise men

Mary

Joseph

Baby Jesus (Baby Doll)

Host of Angels (Girls & Boys)

Props: one gold box, one decorative box of frankincense,

one decorative box of myrrh

Image of a bright star shining from the projector or extra

large shiny star

Costumes

First Wise Man	blue and gold long-sleeve tunic with matching sleeveless over coat, blue and gold pillbox hat
Second Wise Man	red and gold long-sleeve tunic with rope around waist, matching head scarf with rope
Third Wise Man	brown and gold or purple and gold, three-fourth length sleeves with long tunic and circular wrap over one shoulder, matching turban
Mary	a simple peasant dress
Joseph	a tunic with pants, a traditional head scarf with a band
Angel on High	pretty, long, white dress, large wings with a gold halo, battery-operated candles
Host of angels (girls)	shiny white gowns, small wings (replicas of the larger wings), gold halos
Baby doll	blanket
Manger	straw
Sleeping bags	two

THE FIRST WISE MAN

The choir opens the play with "Joy to the World." A solo, "Oh, Holy Night," follows.

The scene begins with the father and his two children, and it is near bedtime.

Father: It's bed time; have you finished brushing your teeth?

Both children: Yes sir, we have.

Father: Alright, off you go. It's Christmas Eve, no presents 'til morning.

Child one: Dad, mom's still out Christmas shopping. Who's going to tell us a story?

Child two: Yeah, Dad. She always tells us a story.

Father: Well, let's see. I'll give you five minutes to get in your bed. Get all tucked in and I will tell you a story. But, you must be tucked in.

The children race off to bed laughing. They are all tucked in when their father enters.

Child One: Where is the book dad?

Child Two: Yeah dad. Mom always reads *The Christmas Story*. You know how the Christ baby was born to Mary and Joseph.

Father: Quiet down (pause). Not tonight guys. Tonight, I will tell the story of the Bright Star.

Both Children: The Bright Star?

Child Two: Is this a true story, Dad?

Father: As true as I can tell it (Dad smiles). Okay, quiet now and let's start the story. Many years ago, there were three young men. The first young man was from a small, poor village. He was known for being smart, kind and helpful. He was a treasure to his parents. Many of the young people had left the village to grow the much-needed crops. The garden needed water. The elders were getting too old to carry the water. The young ones were too weak to push the wheel barrels. As the young man saw how desperate his village needed the crops, he prayed and asked for guidance. As he slept, a vision came to him. He awoke with a plan and developed what is now known as an irrigation system to water and help crops grow. The villagers were so happy that they gave him a small box of gold. As time passed, the young man matured into a wise man. As he slept one night, a vision of a bright star (ANGEL STANDS, STAR APPEARS) appeared to him with an angel beckoning for him to come. He left his village to find the bright star.

An angel is standing at the top of the choir loft, raising the star and beckoning for the first wise man. The first wise man appears at the front of the sanctuary, then moves half-way down the aisle and stands.

The star fades; the angel sits down.

THE SECOND WISE MAN

Father: The second young man came from a village near the sea. Fish was the main staple. All the men owned a fishing pole to provide the main dish of fish for their family. As the young man grew, he noticed that the widows depended on the generosity of the village elders for their fish. Some of these widows were young but had never owned a fishing pole or knew how to use one. Watching the widows wait for leftovers made him sad. As he entered the small chapel in his village he prayed, "Father how can I help these widows feed themselves?" As he slept that night, the vision of a cloth with small holes appeared and was thrown out into the sea. A string was used to pull it back and fish overflowed. Over the next weeks, he practiced until he had a cloth with small holes like in his vision. He tossed it on the water. He waited, then pulled back and found an abundance of fish. He taught the young widows to fish with the cloth and the young widows fed the older widows. The eldest widow gave the young man a fragrant box of frankincense.

As he slept that night, the young man had a vision of a bright star (ANGEL STANDS, STAR APPEARS) with an angel beckoning for him to come. He too left his village in search of this bright star.

An angel standing at the top of the choir loft raises the star and beckons for the second wise man. The second wise man appears at the front of the sanctuary, and then moves half-way down the aisle.

The star fades as the angel sits down.

THE THIRD WISE MAN

The father begins the scene by speaking to his children.

Father: Are you sleepy? Do we need to finish the story tomorrow?

Both children: No, we are not sleepy (as they yawn).

Father: Okay. Well, the third young man lived in a village of scholars. These scholars recorded history in books. The young man also recorded in the scholarly books, but he was known to constantly disappear. The elders often found him near the caves building things, and he was berated for being lazy. The history of the village recorded that every 50 years a monstrous storm from the sea blew through and destroyed the village. As the young man laid down in the cave, he pulled a small cross from his pocket. As he kissed the cross, he asked for understanding from God. "Why am I different?" He soon drifted off to sleep. As he slept, a vison appeared of a strong wall blocking wind and rain. The young man begins the next day gathering large stones and building a wall to protect the village. Although he was laughed at and ridiculed, he continued to build the wall he saw in his vision. When the storm came, everyone and everything survived. The elders recorded the event for history. The young man was considered wise for his time and he was presented with a gift of myrrh. The third young man has a vision of a bright star as he sleeps, **(Angel stands, star appears)** with an angel beckoning him to come. The next day, he leaves his village in search of the bright star.

The angel remains standing at the top of the choir loft holding the star, beckoning high.

The third wise man appears at the front of the sanctuary. All three walk slowly toward the Newborn King to kneel. Angel remains standing, but stops beckoning when wise men reach the Newborn King.

Song: "We Three Kings"

The Wise Men begin slowly heading toward the altar. Joseph, Mary and Baby Jesus join the cast down front. Hosts of angels gather on each side of Mary and Joseph.

The Three Wise Men walk down front and kneel to the Newborn King to present their gifts.

Song: "Who Would Imagine a King?" (solo by a female between the ages of 10-16) or "Angels, We Have Heard on High" (alternative)

Father: This is how the Three Wise Men found the bright star that led them to Bethlehem, to a manger that held our Lord and Savior, Jesus Christ.

Lights are dimmed and candles are raised by the cast.

Everyone, including the congregation, sings the final song.

Song: "Silent Night"

THE END

Acknowledgements

I would like to thank my parents, Mr. and Mrs. John Earl Miller, Sr., for instilling God, family and a great work ethic in my soul. Many thanks to Reverend Dr. Marcel Bush and the Majority Baptist Congregation for believing that this book was possible. I'm grateful for my children and grandchildren whom I love beyond words and finally, but never last, my sister Sherry, my rock, my confidant and the best person I have ever known.

Ms. Ndanyi can be contacted at pndanyi@hotmail.com and welcomes feedback, questions, speaking or poetry reading invitations, bulk sales orders and more.

Lee Anthony Williams, Cover Illustrator, is on Facebook as Black Byrd, and can be contacted at oddball37@ymail.com.

Hadassah's Crown Publishing, LLP

For information about publishing opportunities, visit www.hadassahscrownpublishing.com or email soncunnlev@gmail.com.

www.ingramcontent.com/pod-product-compliance
Lightning Source LLC
Chambersburg PA
CBHW050444010526
44118CB00013B/1675